Aoife Staunton is six years old and lives in Oxford. She likes fairies, colouring and watching *Jem and the Holograms*. This is her first book.

Gabriel Rosenstock (born 1949) is an Irish writer who works chiefly in the Irish language. A member of Aosdána, he is poet, playwright, haikuist, tankaist, essayist and author/ translator of over 180 books, mostly in Irish. Born in Kilfinane, County Limerick, he currently resides in Dublin.

Michel Jovet practises escape from everyday life near Paris, France through writing, recording songs, listening to a lot of metal, and watching a lot of horror movies.

Bang

WORLD SOUNDS

Aoife Staunton

with translations into Irish by Gabriel Rosenstock
and into French by Michel Jovet

The Onslaught Press

Published in Oxford by The Onslaught Press
11 Ridley Road, OX4 2QJ
October 2, 2016

ISBN: **978-0-9956225-5-5**

Typeset in by Jiyukobo's **Hiragino Gothic Pro** on the inside,
and Marcelo Magalhães Pereira's **Londrina** on the cover,
designed & edited by **Mathew Staunton**

Printed and bound by Lightning Source

for my family
and friends

...silence of shooting stars..............

.................ciúnas na réaltaí reatha.

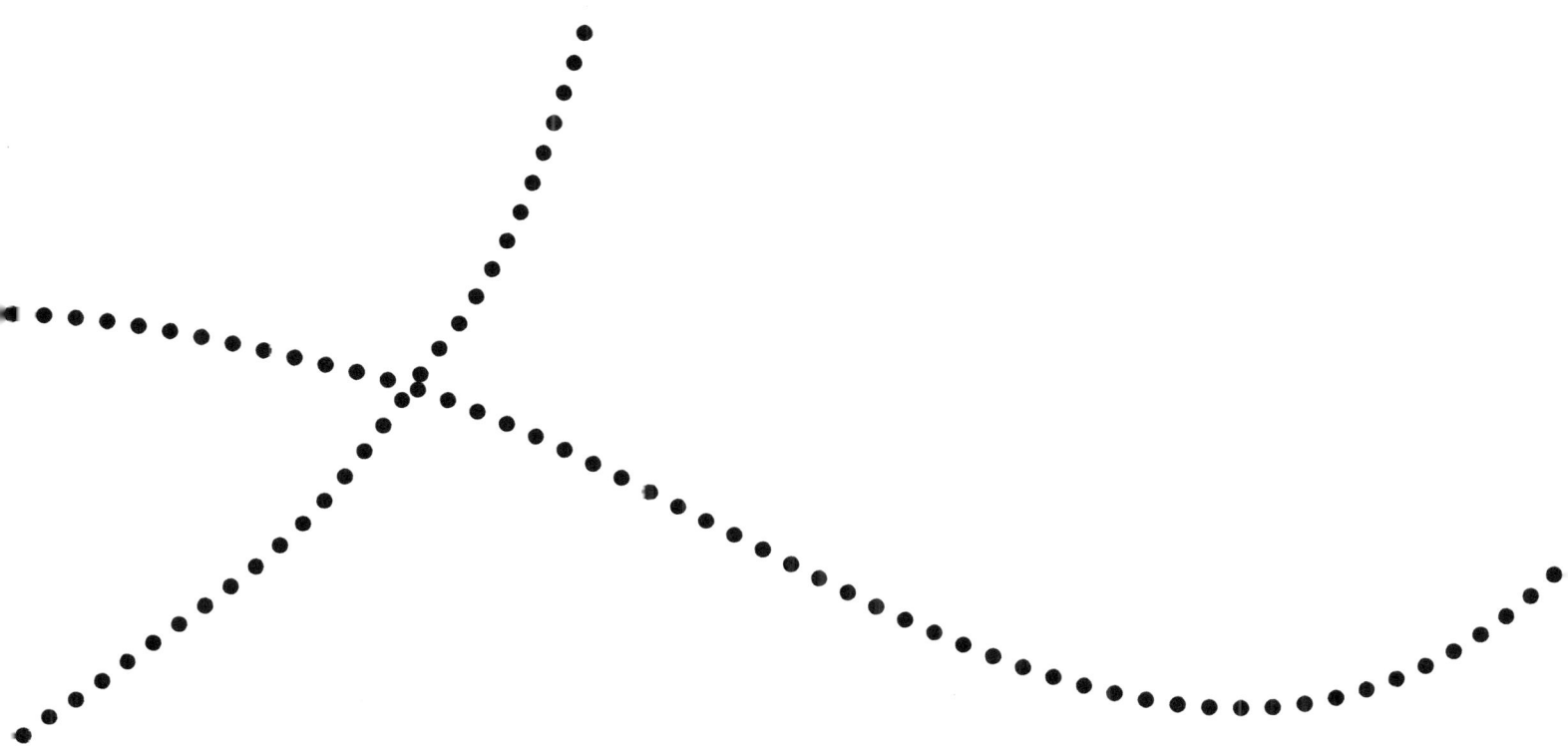

...le silence des étoiles filantes·········

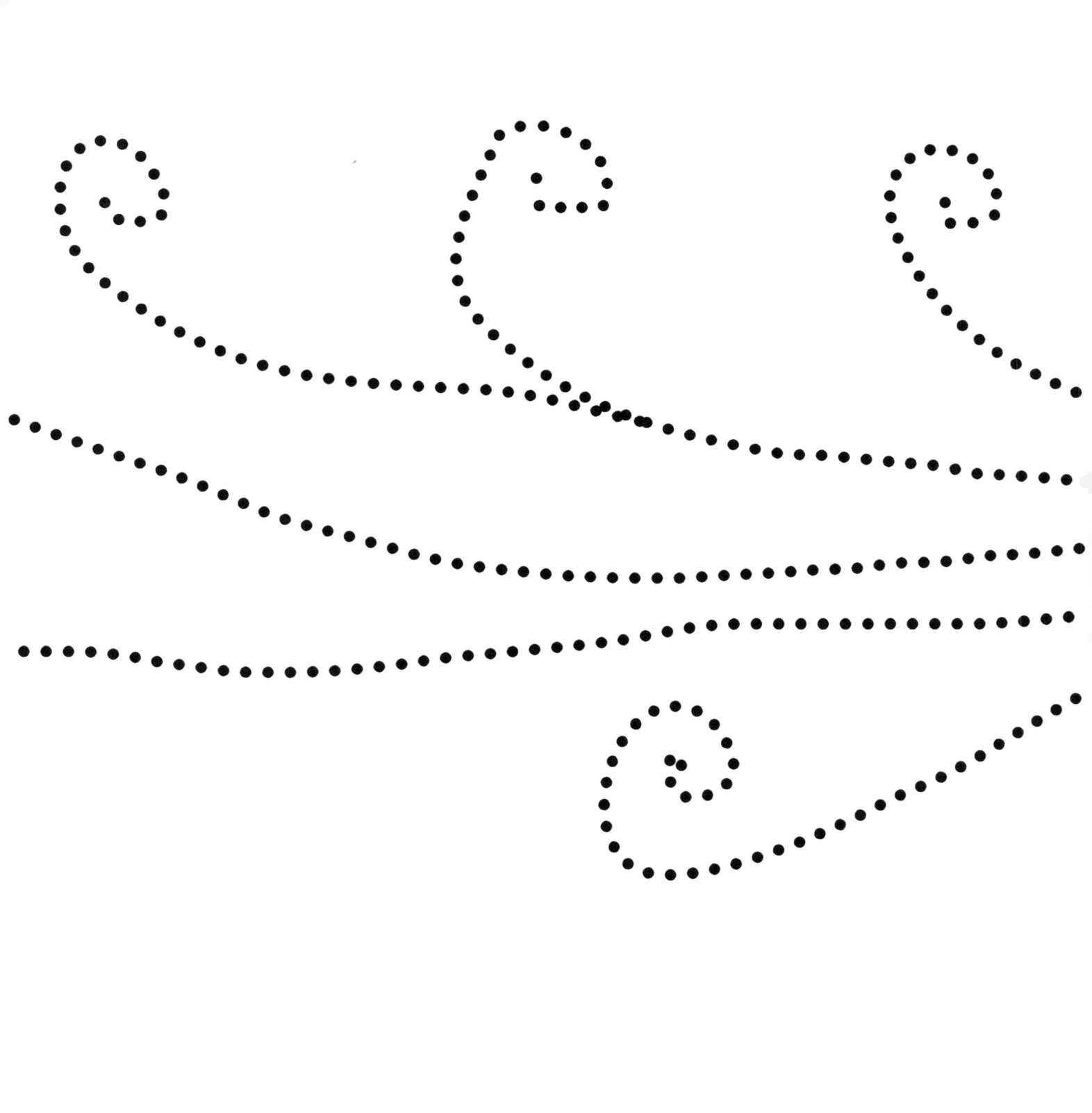

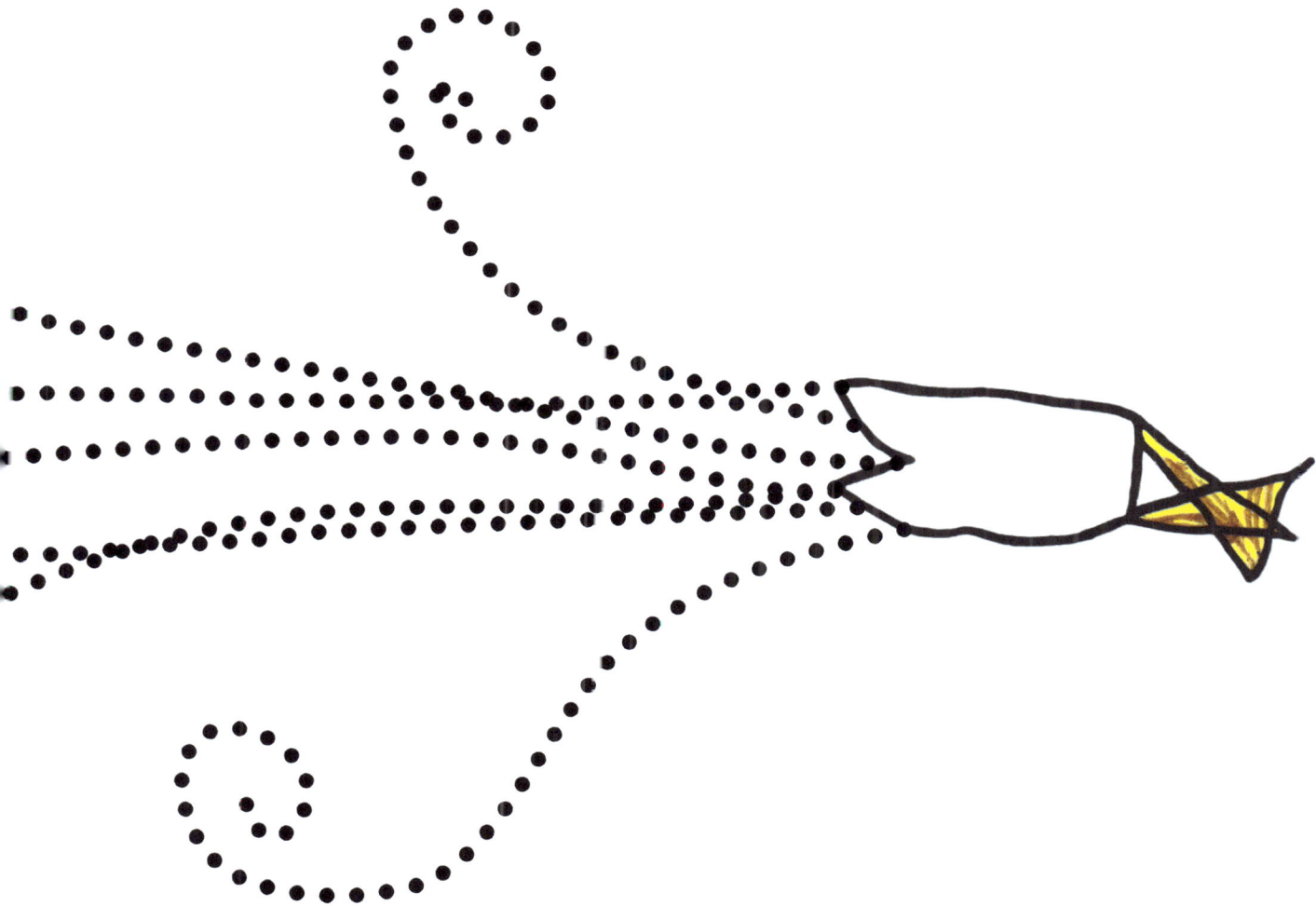

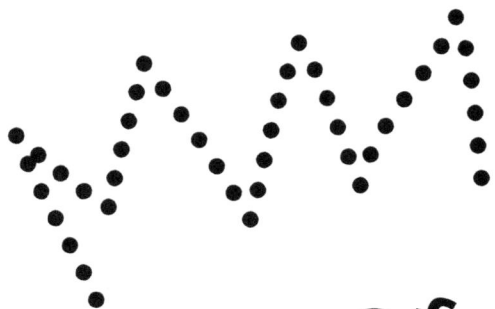

noise of cars

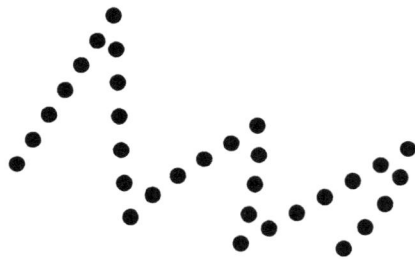

tormán na ngluaisteán

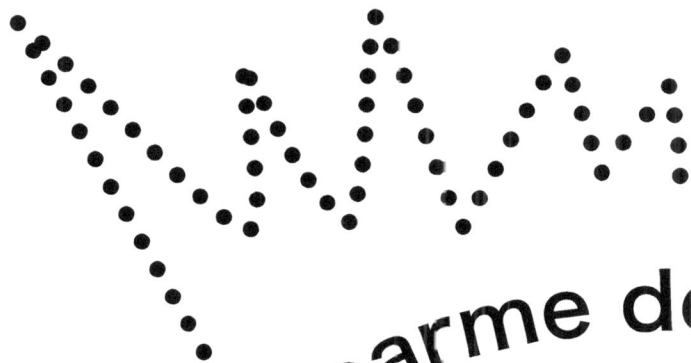

le vacarme des voitures

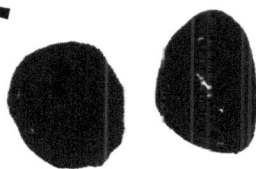

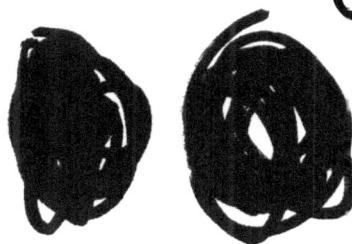

soft songs of birds

cantain shéimh na n-éan

le doux chant des oiseaux

loud clatter of
something falling!

Bang

turlabhait: rud éigin ag titim!

Bang

de quelque chose qui tombe !

le bruyant fracas

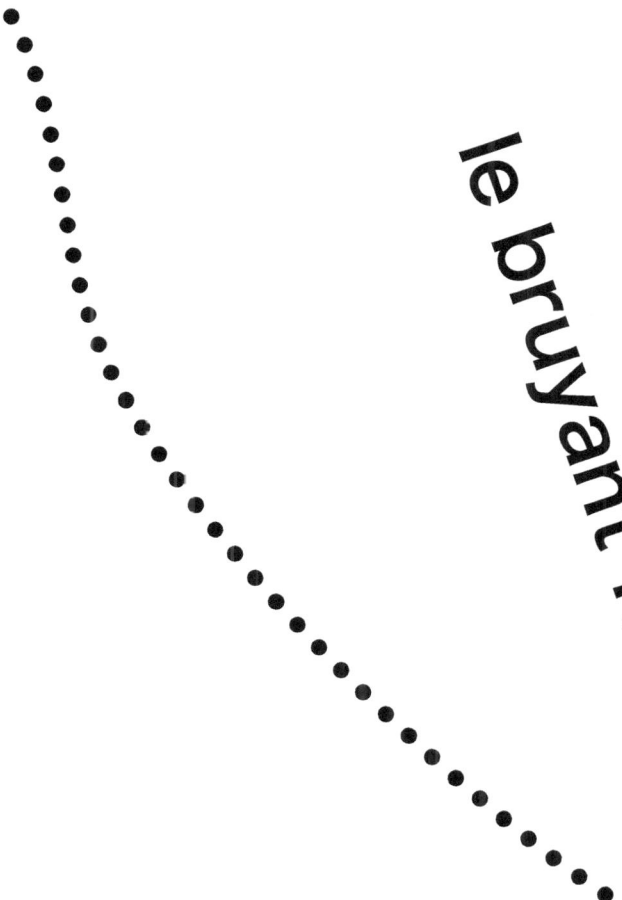

Bang

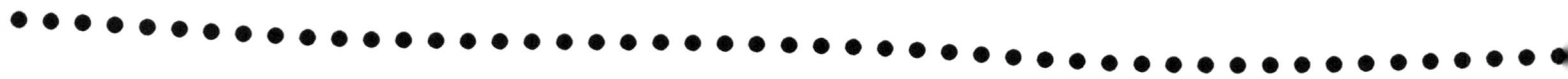

Bang

Une légère brise qui fait chanter les arbres...... a soft breeze makes the songs of trees...

...is í an leoithne bhog a bhog a chruthaíonn amhráin na gcrann

roaring waves at the beach

...le rugissement des vagues à la plage......

......búir na dtonn cois trá......

silence:of flowers growing

ciúnas:na mbláthanna ag fás

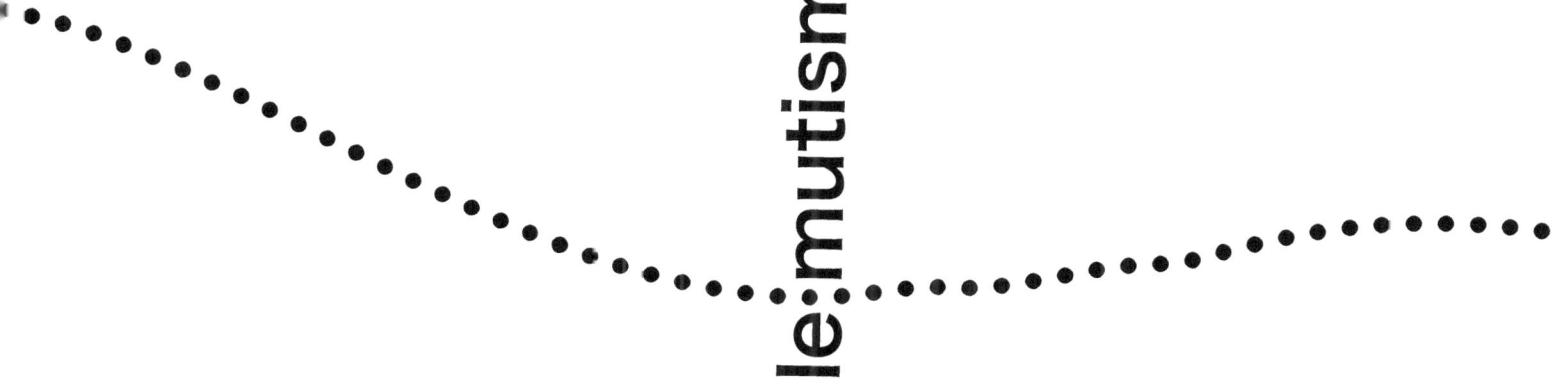

le:mutisme des fleurs qui poussent

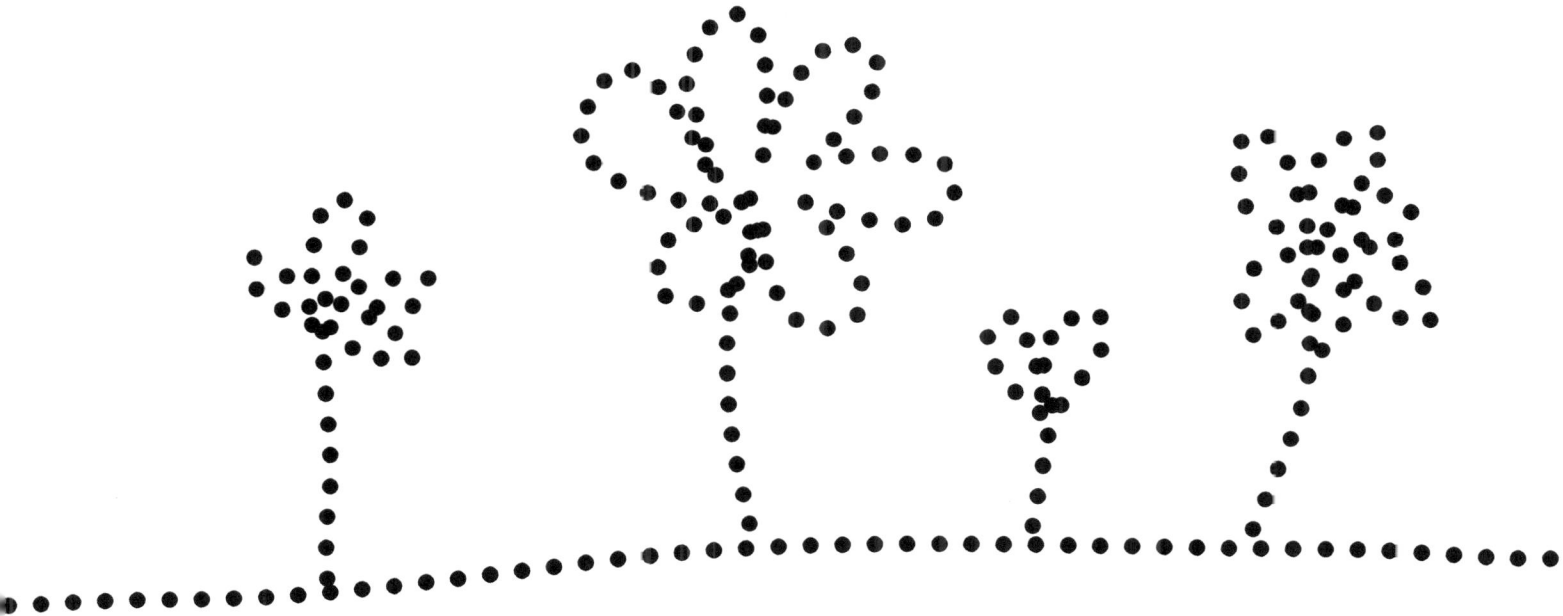

stomping hooves of a pony

Bang

trup trup: crúba an chapaillín

Bang

le piétinement des sabots

d'un poney

Bang

Bang

Bang

Bang

Bang

Bang

other titles from The Onslaught Press

Out of the Wilderness (2016) by Cathal Ó Searcaigh
with an introduction and translations by Gabriel Rosenstock

You Found a Beating Heart (2016) Nisha Bhakoo

ident (2016) Alan John Stubbs

I Wanna Make Jazz to You (2016) Moe Seager

Tea wi the Abbot (2016) Scots haiku by John McDonald
with transcreations in Irish by Gabriel Rosenstock

Judgement Day (2016) Gabriel Rosenstock

We Want Everything (2016) Moe Seager

to kingdom come (2016) edited by Rethabile Masilo

The Lost Box of Eyes (2016) Alan John Stubbs

Antlered Stag of Dawn (2015) Gabriel Rosenstock,
with translations by Mariko Sumikura & John McDonald

behind the yew hedge (2015) Mathew Staunton & Gabriel Rosenstock

Bumper Cars (2015) Athol Williams

Waslap (2015) Rethabile Masilo

Aistear Anama (2014) Tadhg Ó Caoinleáin

for the children of Gaza (2014)
edited by Mathew Staunton & Rethabile Masilo

Poison Trees (2014) Philippe Saltel & Mathew Staunton